Pages of Life

Pages of Life

A Poetry Collection

Written by Calvin D. Morris

The most powerful words come from the mouths of those who believe in them; those who have turned the pages of life and understand how important they are.

Copyright © 2019 by Calvin D. Morris

All rights reserved. No part of this book may be reproduced or used in any manner without written permission of the copyright owner.

No part of this book may be stored in a retrieval system, or transmitted electronically, mechanically or by any other means without written permission of the publisher.

Art and images by Calvin D. Morris

ISBN 978-1-7339232-3-1
Influimage Publishing 2019

To the people who fed and encouraged me when I was homeless — Pages of Life, I owe to you.

Every life has its own birth, so every poem in the Pages of Life has its own formal intro.

Intro

Some of us see people for who they really are, but some of us don't. I don't know why that is, but what I do know is that sometimes people see what they want to see, and when they can't see that, they pretend like they didn't see anything at all. The worst people in the world to me, are those who pretend like they didn't see what they know they saw.

Anastasia

I was a superhero when I was five,
With my mother's eyes and my father's pride,
My name was Teresa, Anna Lisa, Marie,
Amanda, Samantha, Latiqua, Shariece
The secret within me he forced me to keep
Week after week, of course in my sleep

He came, he touched, he needed so much
No blame, no fuss, I loved mother so much,
He'd take her away, he'd kill her he'd say,
I'm probably the reason she's living today

I was a superhero when I was five,
With my mother's eyes and my father's pride,
My life was blue, but she hadn't a clue
Because people do things
You wouldn't imagine they'd do.

Intro

There's nothing wrong with putting your all into a relationship, especially when you're in love with someone that is truly worth loving. I learned that from the most beautiful woman in the world, just before she became my everything.

The Essence of Everything

The misty sky before a busy night
Is all I see with you
All I do is feel for you
Feel for you is all I do

The storm and the rain defines your pain
The rain defines your pain
Your mind is the rain, the rain is insane
Insane when it comes to me

I am what I am because you are what you are
And you are what we are together
The scent from the leaves as the rain hits the trees
Is the freshness I feel with you
What I feel with you is the freshness of the leaves
The leaves are the days of my life

The grass is where I stand with my hand in your hand
To my ankles anchored in your life
Your life is the grass, the reason for my fast
As I travel through lands unconquered
Unconquered and free like your feelings for me

Your feelings for me - are free

Free as in satisfaction, free as in love
Love as in the company of two
Two as in one, but one as in two
Similar to man and nature
And the nature of this - is the essence of everything
And everything my darling - is the essence of you.

Intro

There's no better place to be than in the presence of a wise man. But for a wise man, the best place to be is in the presence of beauty. There's nothing more beautiful to a wise man than two stars in the eyes of a queen.

Dinner with a wise Man
as a wise Man sees a Star

Open my mind and sip fine wine

and watch time rewind back to a time

when a divine love and stars aligned -

and a wise man knew it was a sign

we define these as the foundations of affirmation,

these conversations of love and understanding, sometimes

abandoned by many of truth

Why lie and deny this time as a time of

new-found love and profound hugs

only debugged by the wishes of

God Himself alone

I say we lean not towards temptation

but conversation's enough to change my station, which is

why I'll follow you with no reservations

fall in love no hesitation, leave home no destination

cause I know what you are

you're my future, my destiny,

my heartbeat, my rhythm,

my joy, my star...

Intro

I pray for those of you who have lost a child. I hurt for you. There's a mother that I think about all the time, but I've never even met her. All I know about her is that she loved her child, and that her child loved her.

Forever

He died holding my hand and I never caught his name, at twenty-five he died, at church on a non-church day, not a church day, at twenty-five he died, his soul made a sound, his loved ones weren't around, he died holding my hand and I never caught his name,

I don't know what to call him, I don't know whom to feel sorry for, but I feel his hand everywhere I go, I can't get away from him, he can't get away from me, yet at twenty-five he died

Intro

If you've ever been out on the ocean in the wrong kind of boat, then you know how it feels to be in love with the wrong person. Sometimes all you want to do is to get back to shore, but the shore you find, might not be the shore you're looking for.

The Breath

I was holding my chest tight,
As tight as a chest could be held
For as long as a chest could be held tight-
And then I saw something that was a must to take in
She moved over my life like wind over the water
By the waves over the sand
She took my life to shore

I was at sea for so long,
For so long I'd swam with sorrow
But comfort she gave my heart and my mind-
She loved me to death, I inhaled her love
And to me she became my breath

But her love went first to her lover at home -
And to me came everything else
Her kisses were so refreshing,
Her love renovated my heart
I told myself it was temporary -
She said we'll never part
She wanted devotion, a love to trust,
She thought it was silly to share

The contradictions won't let me rest,
This love was too hard to bare.

For love I took a foolish breath,
With pollution in the air
Like cancer caused by second-hand smoke, the Damage
Defeated my cares

Intro

If I told you that one letter accidentally fell out of the alphabet, you probably wouldn't believe me. But I know it's true because I see evidence of it everywhere I go. I see intelligent people who know what love is, but don't know how to speak it.

The lost Letter

The letter Love was in the language of Lust,
Silently lurking – longing to be learned,
Waiting to lecture the loneliest lover,
Laboring long to maintain its luster,
But lately, Love has meant less to the locals,
Less than lucrative – no longer a luxury,
Lust is logical, but Love is loathsome,
Love is patient though many oppose him,
Through lunacy Love has been loosed and lost,
A costly decision indeed,
For the lonely lack the mental capacity,
To learn the letters they need,
So lovers lay with a broken language,
Only halfway spelling their needs,
They scream for Love in the language of Lust,
And Love knows just when to leave.

Intro

When a King has a Queen, and a Queen has a King, life is truly worth living. To them, Eternity is like one day of a week. Time only extends itself when one is without the other.

Eternity

Eternity is nothing to a king without a queen
One with a voice and no song to sing,

If I could kiss my queen all covered in quilts,
Calmly caress her cunning lips,
Call her precious, keep her mine,
Eternity would be fine.

Eternity is lonely for a man without a wife
One with a heartbeat and still lacking life
One with a past, only to make him sad
Wishing for someone he know he can never have

If I could sing a song to someone special,
Spare the space till another level,
Sacrifice, make her my wife,
Eternity would be nice.

To a man that has a simple soul,
A complex heart, a mind of gold,
A song to sing, a woman of spring,
Eternity is everything.

To me, you are eternity,
Laced with roses, covered with beauty,
Adored by silver, loved by gold,
Hot like fire that heats the cold,
With eyes like diamonds fit for a king
To me, you are everything.

Intro

Even the best relationships can crumble after a few harsh words and a little bit of time to think about them. When you say something that you can't take back, it's best to do what the criminals do, and throw yourself on the mercy of the court.

Magnificent Cup

Don't rush through life
You might fall off the moon
So soon my doom introduces my tomb
This wound so fatal to this heart of mine

Don't curse my mind with words of rhyme-
Confine my time like love is blind,
Find my flashlight, hold it tight
Rewrite my life and spell it right

On site tonight's a desperate fight
But love is like a wall of knights
That fight all night to make it right

Don't leave my life to a feeble few
Why spill my wine when I drink of you?
So new my cave, I know I've played
Put away my game for this ace of spades
Mysterious ways do love invade
Yet save my heart for majestic prey

Magnificent cups in time give up

So find my fountain, drink it up

My mountain less than a grain of seeds
Believe and cross my land of needs

At least forgive me, save me sorrow
Tell me you'll love me again tomorrow.

Intro

I feel so lost when I'm around people who chase relationships like there's no tomorrow. I'm talking about people who go from one relationship to the next, just because they're afraid to be alone.

Lost near the Lonely

I feel your love, it's oh so grand,
But bland to a man who fails to understand
That love's a breeze from a magical fan
That turns your focus, strengthens your plan

Oh so precious is time and swift,
Lift your spirit, command your drift
Time is wasted chasing the truth,
The truth is faithful - it chases you

Hearts are lonely when hearts are broken
Hearts are safe until hearts are opened
Why not rest until love is tested,
Why not pause until love confesses

Name your cost, if I could spare it,
Yes I'd give you a ring and carat
But you need more, and I'm so lost
Cause I can't help you demand your cost

Intro

Some things deserve to be celebrated, like for example the great man that supports you every day. Celebrate him for continuing to love you, even when you're not easy to love.

About Yesterday, Today

Shine bright -
Because tonight's the night to excite the knight
That changed your life to out-of-sight
That made it right, that gave it life
That gave his fight with all his might

That stood for you when you were new
Back when you were barely you
Back when two was barely two
Just cause you were half-a-you

Now tonight's a special night
Some delight for Mr. Right
Something nice to shine a light
On what he did to your delight

Need a reason - take a look
Think of him and what it took
To be with you when you were not
To think of you when you forgot

Intro

There's nothing quite like being in love and still being lonely. It's hard to put a finger on the reason why, but if I had to guess, I would say that it's because love is a feeling that should never be paired with loneliness.

Sleeping without a Wife

The move she made created distance –
Emotional space in the face of need,
A spit and spatter in the face of love –
In disregard for what it was,
Left my marriage without a chance,
Left my song without a dance,
Now my heart has frozen up,
Now my eyes have opened up,
Time to go from to to fro –
Let me know if you can go,
So I can be in better hands –
Do you really love a man,
Do you really understand,
Do you know when freedom rings,
Freedom rings when people sing –
Sing aloud and I am yours,
Dance with me and open doors –
Thought I was forever hers,
But I can be forever yours

Intro

The truth is that I'm afraid of myself, more so than I am anyone else. My mind is so volatile and fragile. It's not the kind of mind that I want to have, but right now, I'm in a position where I can't even control my own mind. It's not my fault though, it's yours.

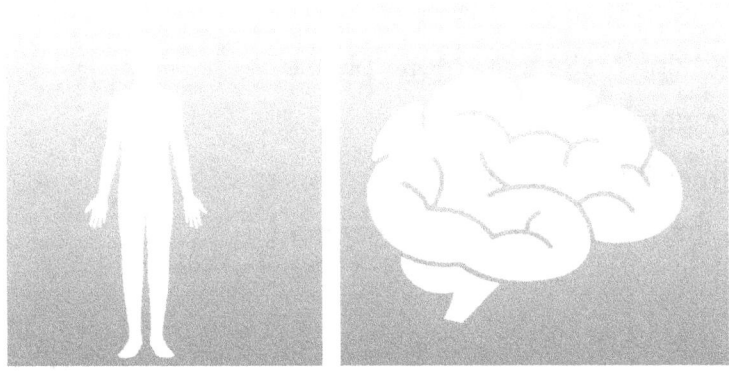

Misconception

I'm not a man of many faces

so people want to hurt me just to see me hurt

I don't break and I don't bend

but I'm scarred and marred, scratched and dented

bruised and battered, used and shattered

I'm hard to read but I'm soft spoken

I'm clever and crafty so people bash me just to see me fall,

I've fallen before so I'm tired and sore

depressed and stiff, my feelings are hurt

my heart can't take it anymore, please

help me get rid of this pain,

if I kill myself they will blame me,

but it's them that are causing the pain

Intro

There's nothing wrong with having a long distance relationship with someone, especially when you can't find what you need in your own area. A friend abroad is better than no friend at all. That's why love has come to life over the always available internet.

Saturation

Specs and pixels, dots and spots
A digital love affair that's heated-hot
Fascination with complications
Glad I'm stationed across the nation
Cause If I wasn't, I'd love to death
Clearly love, she loves the best

I found a fountain to stir my youth
To tell the truth she's better than you
Computer screens fulfill my dreams
A brand new team for me to lean
Steamy showers in the after-hours
A fight for power as we do ours

What we do is in a perfect hue
What you do is a perfect you
But I know me, and I need more
So I don't rush to touch the door
I just bathe in saturation -
Share myself across the nation

Intro

If you've never met anyone that took your breath away, then you might not understand this one. But if you have, then you know just how blown away you can be by the right person at the right time.

And You

...and You

...and you are like spring water flowing over my life

Like precious diamonds in a beam of light

A blinding beauty so fine and truly

A timeless piece like wine or rubies

...and you

...and you are like flakes of gold or hints of treasure

In any case a sign of pleasure

A way to love like God above

A guiding light like stars at night

...and you

...and you are like a magic potion for a desired emotion

An emotional high like joy multiplied

A perfect gift in an imperfect world

Immersed in beauty like a perfect pearl

...And you.

Intro

Love is not like it used to be. Things have changed. The way we used to love doesn't exist anymore, at least that's what I believe. Nowadays, saying I love you is the same as saying hi when you walk by someone on the streets.

Today's Market

Roses are red, violets are blue –
Gist of the things we used to do
Hour glasses, making passes
Hand in marriage, always asking
Yes I love you meant forever
Would I leave you, never ever
Simple changes by simple people
Who say they love, but never keep you
Say they trust, but never know you
Say they lead, but never show you
Today's market is full of phonies
Who say they love but leave you lonely
This is why I'm in a rush
To see my ashes - dust to dust

Intro

Two wrongs don't make a right. I know that, you know that and so does just about everyone else. Yet there are times when we allow our pain to turn us into monsters, and monsters always forget that two wrongs don't make a right.

Vigilante

You might say it was a justifiable homicide, or just another day when the junkie died, but justice just don't step aside for jive turkeys who like to joke and jive, the judges talk about jurisdiction, while the jury juggles facts and fictions, the jungle don't like to wait for justice, justice just don't cut the mustard, Jim and Drew thought Judy forgot, but Judy's nightmares never stopped, first she called up Jack and Jacob, Jacob had some sins to make-up, so justice came with a face of fury, even after the judge and jury, then she called up John and James, James don't really play no games, justice came again and again, just when Jim thought the pain would end, just when Judy thought the pain would stop, justice handed her name to cops

Intro

I admire those who fall in love at first sight, but that's not always how it happens. Some of us go through many relationships trying to find that special someone to share the rest of our lives with.

Dissatisfaction

Sit down,
and feel the terror and horror in the area of love
your insight was right, and the thought of it is the ghost that
hunts your heart

The murder weapon is trapped in your spirit
your spirit is now a victim of love's most dangerous foe, an
unsure lover - a knight and adversary on the field of battle
the field is within your temple, the temple is the body

The most precious areas are the mind and heart -
even the soul can be influenced by knights
a powerful knight has entered your mind
and poisoned your every thought

Your mind was battered
your heart was shattered
now stand up and be a person!

Intro

They say every king must fall, and every life has its peaks and valleys, but rejoice during your peaks and show no weakness while in your valleys....

Eyes of the Conquered

So great was his sword, his shield, his strength
His men, his might, his plan—
He strapped on his armor with pride, with honor
Much power he held in his hand—
His demeanor was frighteningly calmer than most
His heart was fearless and bold—
His battles were swift, his enemies he slew,
His stories, they never grew old—
But tales of a warrior more feared than he
Had swiftly covered his land
And time, and time, and time again
He was forced to hear of the man—
Since he who battles must battle again
Til one can disprove his might,
He dressed in his armor as always before
For speed his armor was light—
He came to The Valley of the Shadow of Death
Covered in the blood of the Lamb
But his enemy saw he had eyes of the conquered,
And realized he was only a man.

Intro

I think everybody should dream big, but it's never a good idea to dream the entire book of dreams at once. Every dream has its season. Perhaps the season you've been waiting for is just around the corner. All you have to do is wait for it to flow down river.

Book of Dreams

Life is like a book of dreams
Trapped in a cave near a red river stream
Tinted by night, brightened by day,
Elevated by spirits, overcome by faith;
Close to the moon paired with the sun,
Cold and calm, yet violent and warm
A one-way roadway, a brand new old day,
So contradictory, but just won't go away

Life is like a book of dreams,
Trapped in a cave near a blue river stream
Filled with tests on right and wrong,
Spiritual enlightenments and angelic songs,
Passionate memories, the open sea,
Beautiful trees with golden leaves,
Life is free, like birds with wings,
A child without destiny, a man with dreams

Life is like a book of dreams
Balanced between two river streams,
Creating for itself a sensible reason,
An explanation for its changing seasons,

A nightmare today, a pleasant fantasy tomorrow,
A minute of happiness, sixty seconds of sorrow,
Life is simply a book of dreams
That keeps us wondering what each day will bring.

Intro

A group of blue birds told me that there's power in numbers, but it's not always good to run with the pack. Your best bet, is to get out when the getting is good. But sometimes you might be better off getting it alone.

Bluebirds

Bluebirds shadowed a shallow land
Ungrateful in fashion for friendly hands
Blown from the section of the sun's rising
To the western section of a fantasy island
Captured by elegance a-somewhat-new
Veiled by riches undoubtedly new

Bluebirds traveled a shallow land
As flightless birds for the jewels at hand
Priceless jewels each of them were
But no one bird could carry a four
All bluebirds ran away with five
Desperate bluebirds, now none could fly
Escape by sky, but none would try

Bluebirds traveled a shallow land
With evidence of a storm by unquestionable hands
No thoughts of a peace that each could reach
At least a tree would spell relief
A storm from hell would cover them all
Ice and hail soon smothered them all
If it seems to easy to gain it all

These bluebirds can explain it all
You live your life with greed and lust,
You'll end your life in greed and lust.

- To the bluebirds of the world.

Intro

When you start believing that everybody has your back, just because they said they have it, that's when you're in big trouble, because when everybody has your back, nobody has your back. Maybe one or two people might be telling you the truth, but the rest of them are lying.

Through the Eyes of an abandoned Few

I see you world, as broken glass
You spilled my hopes and dreams
And many came with towel in hand
To wipe the floor so clean

I see you world, as Captain Crook
You sent me out to sea
You taught me how to pull the anchor
But not to sail the sea

I see you world, as sour grapes
You gave my face a frown
You know I love to eat your fruit
But yet you break me down

You saw me once in need of help,
You pulled your hand away
But yet you want to take the credit
For where I stand today

I see you world, as tented glass
I barely see your intentions
So when I find success in life
It's you I'll barely mention, see ya!

Intro

The angels in heaven are with us. They believe in us. They do everything they can to make sure we are a couple of pure power. Because of them we are a wonderful and remarkable couple.

The Seven Wonders of the World

When I look in your eyes I see butterflies that land on piles of sand, sat down by angel men, flew in from heaven to make the seven wonders exist

Your heart is like a cup of gold placed on a table by angel women, who wrote the beginning of love for many, I remember taking a sip of your soul from the cup of gold that no man could hold and it froze my soul and lit the world

Curls of romance and lovely chants wrapped the planets and made them dance, a chance for love to be born again, your naked skin remains the origin of every existing thing, they sing songs that leave your mouth as galaxies without stars about, let out by God as precious dew, to fall on you and make love come true

Two piles of sand advanced with the wind, blew away by angel men and women complete, your beautiful eyes flew away from the piles for many many miles to landed on my heart with diamond feet, one touch of your feet and my heart started to beat, giving me the elements of understanding

Me landing on your table of happiness sparked the first fire the world had ever seen, people raced over the green to see things that they had only dreamed, we bring things to this world, unbelievable things, things seen only by kings and queens as everyday things, the seven wonders of the world

Your heart, my heart, your soul, my soul, your smile, wisdom and understanding, the seven wonders of the world

Intro

After you hurt the person that you care about the most, you only have one option, and that's to own up to it. No matter how great of a friend you think you are, every once in awhile you will disappoint one of your friends. When you do, the mist will cover the window. Be ready for it.

The Mist that covered the Window

As the moon released the sky,
and the sun drew it in,
the clouds became consistently grey,
and hid the sky within,

And a mist began to cover the window;
thick, and completely grey,
the view was suddenly gloomy-like, and light had gone away,

As I reached up and touched the window,
away my finger sprung,
the mist began to bubble up,
and water began to run,

The water's trail told an amazing tale,
as it went down that window pane,
the trail became so suddenly clear,
like sunshine after rain,

Within the mist was a wounded eye,
and the eye had shed a tear,

the love that use to comfort my heart, I watched it disappear,

How dare he hurt perfection;
this reckless hand of mine,
cast him out into a lonely place,
where a friend, he shall never find.

Intro

Be careful whom you choose. The wrong pick might be a bad decision that never corrects itself. Life is far too short to spend it trying to correct a bad decision. Get out while you can. Love is not worth the pain you feel when you can't get back the love you give.

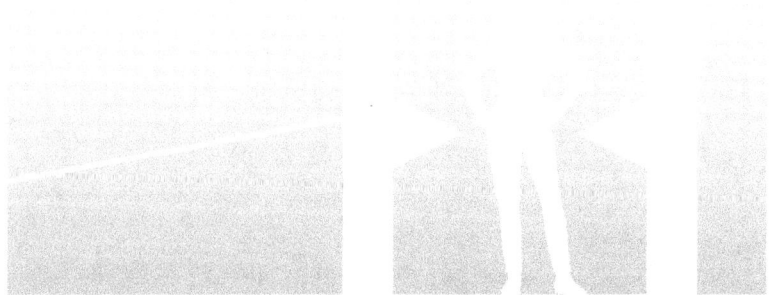

The Thorn in my Side

I should have a crown on my head,
But instead, I have a thorn in my side
My love is insufficient - her greed is tremendous
I can't get away - but why?

If I played you a tune, it would pop your balloon
And again, away you would fly,

You would tell me I'm wrong - try to play me a song
But if it helped me - I'd be surprised

As a leader - I lead, but my love don't believe,
It hinders and strangles my success
My best has been given, but why won't she listen
Others would have loved me for less

A wife is a crown when her husband's around
But this one, she's bringing me down

Whom should I blame for this heartache and pain
This burden that forces my frown

With this pain that I'm feeling, this name I was given
May never survive such shame
It seems that forever I'm stuck with this thorn
When I picked her, I picked up the blame

Intro

You know she's special when you can count on her to ease your pain. No matter how hard your heart has become, there's always a flower that can soften it up. If you have one, then you know what I mean.

The Heart that grew a Flower

There was a heart that knew no love,
That had no life, that knew no wife
That kept no pain, and felt no shame,
That felt no shame and felt insane
Now that's my pain, it slept within
My sun it came, but left again
It rained and rained and wet my skin
Lord help my heart, it died again
He held my hand and I cried again
My sun came in and I tried again

I knew a friend that knew a power
That touched my heart and it grew a flower
An hour passed and life went on,
My showers came back and life went wrong,
So I opened my heart and grabbed my flower
And began to thank God that I had my flower
You could see my smiles inside my eyes
As I snatched my flower out and it dried my skies

I thanked that God because he gave me you
I thanked that God because you made me new

You grew and you grew and you made me true
And that's what a woman was made to do—

The love of a woman, in the life of a man…

Intro

We are not born to bury our children, so my heart hurts for him and her. To those who murdered her, I hope the weight of the world comes crashing down on you. I hope God shows you mercy, but only after you've paid for your crime. I can't stay silent anymore, so there.

Just after Five

Pronounced dead at five seventeen
her cries never heard through her mother's screams
forever muted in a Chicago shooting
Michigan child with a worldwide smile

dead at twelve the ground covered in shells
she was tightly held as the community failed
too many cases in the pages of life
with the same old pain, with the same old strife

Intro

She exploded into my life with love and excitement. From the very beginning, I couldn't resist her. Her charm, her smile and her big brown eyes were everything I wanted in a woman. The fireworks in her eyes showed me just how beautiful life with her could be. My girl. My woman. My life.

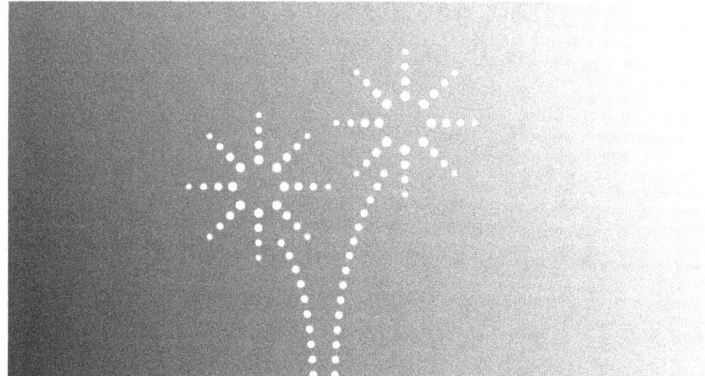

The Fireworks in the Sky

The fireworks in the sky remind me of the first time I saw your face, at the time I was thinking you could be my soul mate.

It reminds me of the first night I realized that I actually had a chance with you, I felt fireworks in my heart, kind of like I was leaving for the most important journey of my life

It was like you blended with the stars
like you joining my life added to what was written in the stars for me

It reminds me of the first time I held you in my arms
I felt this peace that said eternity,
that said forever,
that said never ending

It reminds me of the first time I looked into your eyes
there was a sparkle
a sparkle that said I am to be loved
I am to be honored

I am to be held

the fireworks in the sky

they remind me

they remind me of you

Intro

You are who you are and you can't change that, even in the face of a man who loves you to death. I learned that from her. She taught me what it's like to fall in love with an independent woman. It's not the worst thing in the world, but it's not the best thing either.

Genus

She went through the best of me with her mental telepathy,
classified me physically as the god of misery, tore me apart from my soul to my heart,
then rejected my passes like the killer of chemistry,

I'm not surprised that she's a spoiler of vibes, must've derived from an original tribe, an emotional species with devotional needs, mentally physical, tough individual, she was unusual just like I was illusional

A traditional man, she could never get use to
serious fallacies in her mysterious twine
she's an imperfect scroll, so tightly rolled
but her beautiful soul has a hold on my mind
faintly aloof, she just can't get a loose
from the equivocal nature of a conditional queen

Intro

Decades later and I still can't talk about it. The pain is still burning inside of my heart and I just can't let it go. One day, I will tell my story.

The Shame

I'll give you some candy he said, as he climbed up on my back, but candy just wasn't good enough, what happened next I forgot

Intro

Sometimes the answer is right in front of your face. You might not see it now, but maybe one day, when the time is right, you will. Be open minded, because the answer might come from the most unlikely source.

Success is in the Apple Trees

First, he looked up high
Then, he looked down low
He said, "Answer me a question"
But the ground didn't know.

So he looked up higher
To the top of the trees
The wind began to blow
In motion went the leaves
The trees began to rock
The leaves began to shake

"If I ask you a question, how long will it take"
But then, an apple fell
Leaving nothing in its place
He looked up at the leaves
He saw an empty space
A tiny space it was
Behind it was a face

He saw the face and fell asleep,
Then he found his way,

Success is in the apple trees,

Way behind the leaves,

Remove the apples, move the leaves

And life is just a breeze.

Intro

When it's beautiful, you know it, because beauty has a way of making itself known. Sometimes a special person comes along that can't be ignored. That's when life becomes like some kind of love poem; one that is as sweet as the person you can't ignore.

Some kind of Love Poem

Your eyes and your face is a beautiful place
For me to look and write some kind of love poem
Your neck and your chest, with all due respect
I'd love to travel and recite some kind of love poem

Your mind and your heart is like an unnamed park
That would be great to sit and read some kind of love poem

Your desire for a kiss and the fire upon your lips
Are very good reasons why you need some kind of love poem

Your indulgence in passion and love's great fashion
Would make my life similar to some kind of love poem
A bright red rose, your heart and your soul
I'd love to include in some kind of love poem

I can look into your eyes, and rub your thighs
With no complaint - as long as it's in some kind of love poem

I can kiss your neck and massage your chest
With no witnesses, as long as it's in some kind of love poem

I would have you mother my child,
make my whole life smile

If we were living in some kind of love poem
Our everyday life, it seems alright,
But damn I wish life was some kind of love poem.

Intro

If I had a dollar for every time a man slipped, I'd be a rich man. Men slip everyday, but there's something to be said about a man who gets caught slipping all the time. That's what I call a dangerous man. Stay away from him. He's not worth your time.

Slipping

He was slipping that's for sure
But she was on a ship headed for shore
She sensed his song from a mile away
But he couldn't sing so she shied away

It's a slippery slope some would say
But since his song was the song of the day
She saved some time for his simple mind
She listened intensely to his second line

He sighted an opening and slipped in slowly
He said something special, he said something holy
She started to smile as he seized the moment
But that's when his ex-girl slipped up on him

She spoke her pease with the worst of words
She said some stuff that he knew he deserved
He dropped his head and abandoned ship
He went much further than a man should slip

Keep on slipping, you better search your scene!
She said that loud, she said that mean

Now back to Molly who left the party
She went back home so melancholy

So surreal when she left the scene
She can't be seen on a sloppy team
Up all night she started to scream
Are you kidding me! Search the scene!

Intro

When it's wrong you know it. You don't need anyone else to tell you that you fell in love with the wrong person. No matter how bad that person wants to hold on, you need to let that person go. It takes courage, but you have to do whatever it takes to move on.

Say no More

She said it was beautiful and I wished her well,
She threw three or four pennies in the wishing well

Which splashed the birds that somehow knew
That this was a dream that would never come true

She sighed aloud as she gazed at the clouds
Amazed by color that drew a crowd

Vowed to love me 'til the day she die,
But I stood silent with no reply

Here's a place we've been before
She looked at me -
She said, "Say no more."

Intro

You can't let them get you down. Haters are everywhere. No matter where you go, haters will always be there trying to find a way to mess up your day. I would encourage you to keep turning the pages. Eventually, they'll realize that you have a new page for every day of your life.

Pages of Life

Why must they judge a book by its cover?
When they can flip through the pages of birthdays and ages,
Read between the lines of statements and phrases, peel
back a Cloud and peak at the sun
Is that too complicated?

As the Table of Content direct them further,
They stumble upon things they've never heard of,
That's when they become so bold

They put bookmarks between my yesterdays,
As though yesterday was not just a day
How could they be so cold?

Some flip to the middle to see what I'm about,
Then rush off hastily running their mouths
I thought they would study me whole,

But they put me down like they've reached the conclusion,
try To come back later but it causes confusion,
Whenever I'm winning, they tell you I'm losing-

How can I reach my goal?

To tell you the truth I don't go crazy,
As readers stop and fold my pages,
After they tell you I've lost my way,
I add to the pages of life.

Intro

I know how it is when you know what you want, but can't find it anywhere. It's hard, but it is what it is. Sometimes your special someone is way on the other side of the galaxy, too far away to be discovered by you. Maybe one day, your worlds will come together, but until then, you should leave your name amongst the stars.

Where is my special Someone?

There he is, somewhere far down the road
Right between fate and fantasy,
Reality and destiny
She is caught up in the tide,
The waves have her drowning in despair
The thorns have surrounded her heart
She has been tainted

He loves himself,
But he hates his life
She has been many times a girlfriend,
But never a wife
His heart is broken
Her heart is cold
His heart is on the map,
But she couldn't find the road

Outside the galaxy there is a star so alone,
He is her special someone
Waiting to come home
Outside the galaxy there is a star so bright,
She is his special someone

The cure to his life

Outside the galaxy love goes astray,
Life is often windy and love blows away,
Outside the galaxy.

Intro

You knew it was wrong before you did it, so for you, the price will be much, much higher. Only those who didn't know any better will receive the lower price. I've paid my price, so now it's time for you to pay yours.

Mountain of Hope

As white tears came down the mountain
Roaring loud as heck,
Shaking knees amounted to fear,
As everyone hit the deck

The foolish fainted and vanished viciously,
As first in line to fail
The wise wrestled to will their destiny,
But fought to no avail

The Christians crumbled and cried to Christ,
But Christ would keep them not,
They cursed and cursed and cursed some more,
But Christ would save them not

And one appeared at the base of the mountain
Stern and strong in faith
He gently touched the mountain's face and
Wiped its tears away

"Powerful mountain with all this force,
You have forced my hand to move,

Take with you the weak in faith,
But hand me back the fools"

The mountain spit and roared aloud,
Its rocks began to dance
For who is he who would lose the rest,
And give a fool a chance-
Unless. . .

Intro

I go through things just like everyone else and so do you. I've been up and I've been down. I've had bad times and I've had the best of times. Misery though, I wouldn't wish on anyone. Misery almost devoured me, but before it could, I got help from someone who knew how to beat it. You should do the same.

I know Misery

I know misery, it loves company
I see signs of what it's done to me
I know misery, it loves battery
It wants to beat me until it shatters me

I know misery, it causes pain
It runs the business of causing shame
I know misery, it made me lonely
It took my beauty and made me homely

I know misery, pass the word
I know some who haven't heard
Some have happiness, some have intimacy
Some know joy, but I know misery

Intro

When I saw her, I could only say three words. You will discover what those words are as you read the poem. I knew the first time I saw her that I would never let her go. It was as clear as day that she and I would be together forever.

As clear as Day

Picture perfect, pretty babe
Precious, priceless loving grace
Lifted like a lily blown
Less than God Himself alone

Elected easily as beauty queen,
Elevates beauty to its fullest extreme
Always prosperous like apple trees
Always adored by other seeds,

Sometimes simple with special needs,
Sometimes labeled the best of breeds,
Even though in this poem you still don't see
Everything that will join you and me…

Many men made many mistakes
Most of us give credit to fate
Allowing the Lord to have His way
Always picturing a better day

Righteous men and women combine

Reliving their lives, as I will mine

Rebuilt in spirit, refined in mind
Revealing the love, tested by time

You can read this poem and it'll still be a mystery
You have two eyes, yet you still don't see…

Most of all, my life is a miracle
Made perfect by a woman from the northern area
Eventually life will remove the veil
Eventually, hopefully, with time, your eyes will tell…

Intro

May God be with you when you are in the presence of people who have no heart: those who have no love for others. Rapists, murderers, thieves, liars and haters all know that I can't stand to be around them. I refuse to be in the presence of those who hurt people, and so should you.

I don't need You

I don't, because I lost all trust in people
The moment he touched me I knew
That the world was full of people like you

So I can't be seen with your kind
Not at six, seven or nine
Not on Monday, Tuesday or any day
Not online, in person or in any way

I can't, because my soul won't let me do it
Your world is way too fluid
Your sins are not my sins
And your friends are not my friends
So I don't, can't and won't, ever need you

Intro

The world might not understand you, but you need to stay true to the mission that God gave you, regardless of what people say. When your world turns upside down, there's no telling what kind of problems will fall in your lap. Heaven awaits you, only if you stay true to the mission.

Mirror to my Soul

Now within these thoughts, my mind switches over
my clover lacking a leaf, my leaf missing a stem
my life so dim, my mirror saying, "Is it him, is it him."

With my heart I see, and with my eyes I feel
as I shed down tears they run up hill
what I feel is real because I'm upside-down in a world of
clowns that tell bad jokes to sad folks with uneven yolks,
even these folks must notice my crown

My sound so loud, my soul so weak,
the meek so sweet, yet seem to sleep
I'm an honest man with a simple goal
to elevate souls on the evil globe

So old my robe and somewhat blue
yet sufficient enough to represent truth
eternity blue, if my angels fly through
and the mirror don't recognize my soul.

Intro

Gossip can ruin even the best of relationships, especially for people who believe everything they hear. It's important to know that there are people out there who take pride in destroying relationships, especially the good ones. You and your relationship might be on their list.

Othella

This Sabbath day is a time of truth,
My ancient queen in this time of youth
A genius king in society's eye,
Yet I know not why my Othella cry

My sky, my land, my open sea
My dream, my life, my fantasy
"Othella, Othella why speak so low?"
"I wrote you a poem." I heard it slow

A poem at which she flung to me
With a glimpse of a tear that sung to me
"Othella, Othella what's wrong with thee?"
When I moved her eyes moved along with me

"I wrote you a poem, I wrote it in red."

I started to wonder why Othella's in bed
Her leg, her leg was from bed to floor
Othella was quiet, but said some more

"You live in a world where lies are known,

Your eyes of love, those eyes are gone
Around this place I've seen you care,
But the people, they tell me they've seen you there
My life is worthless like the breaths I take,
It's no mistake! It's no mistake!
I wrote you this poem to show my love,
What I feel is love, what you feel is not love,
I wrote you a poem, a poem in red"

Those were the last words my Othella said
Her poem was in blood, she died on me
Othella, Othella who lied to thee!

My love is true, my love is true,
My love! My love Othella!
Othella!

Intro

The darkest days of his life were spent in the lighthouse. It's ironic I know, but it's true. His best moments were shared with the captain of The Highlighted Flower-Ship, Mrs. Hung, who came to see him at least once a month.

Highlighted Flower-Ship

It sailed like a ship of peace, floating across the sea beneath
brightened by sun rays as the soul on Sundays,
the holiest day of the week

Enchanting melodies escaped its lips
and joyfully drew nigh to me

For one second of time, the light that's mine
advanced its beauty and passed

Of all the blessings mine eyes did see,
this beauty is the beauty most scholars did speak
directed to me, purposefully set within my destiny

I feel as a king with the greatest of things,
a soul-mate to be and to be

Ownership forever, to be and to be
Highlighted Flower-Ship now closer to me

My statue is greater foundation to head,

her love is happy or courageous instead

My tower she approached with the best of her trust,
and monthly I satisfied her needs

No doubt in mind, in heart and soul,
my flower-ship will return to me
with trust unknown to all the masses,
in this I do believe.

Intro

You don't need a doctor to tell you that you're getting old. All you have to do is wake up and do what you've always done. The time it takes to do the simple things will tell you everything you need to know. Getting old is a luxury that should be embraced and enjoyed. So I would encourage you to live life to the fullest, every chance you get.

Almost Gone

Would you rather be a lonely lady for a simple reason,
Or a lonely man in a plentiful season

Time is bleeding, life is speeding,
It's no secret my hair is receding

I'm in a zone of danger, a world of anger
Uncontrolled on a dynamic angle

The birds in trees look down on me
The golden years put a frown on me

If I just had love, I could smile again
If I had one chance, I'd be wild again

If I just had love, I'd be young again
Give me a chance to sing the song again

I'm a lonely man in a plentiful season
Time is bleeding, life is speeding…

I live my life with one great fear

Will I pass away in the upcoming year

If I just had love – I'd be secure,
If I just had love, I'd still be here

If I just had love, I'd still be here,
If I just had love…

Intro

For those of you who are chasing peace, the light is waiting for you. No matter how lost you think you are, there's still a little bit of light left in the darkness. Be not ashamed of what you're going through, because anyone can get lost on a path filled with darkness. Rest assured that love will find a way to get you out.

The Hunt for Peace and the joyful Light that loves It

There is a Light that shines in the darkness, and Darkness himself knows not why
if you hold on to the Light while walking in darkness and shine it on wisdom, wisdom will come in to you

In the Light there is knowledge, and knowledge is the pathway to wisdom
one needs to understand to find wisdom and wisdom to find understanding
understanding shall carry you to perseverance and perseverance to everlasting life

There is a Love that shines through hate and hate understands not why
if you throw this Love in the face of hate, hate will reveal its inner secrets
these secrets shall come to the Light, and the Light will call them truth

Truth is the reflection of Love, and Love is the reflection of truth a reflection of a reflection is an honest reflection, and the truth about the truth is the truth.

There is a Joy that knocks on the door of anger, and anger hates to answer
anger is only a temporary resident, but longs to be a permanent owner
if Joy was to bring war, anger would answer, but Joy brings peace instead

The rejection of peace is a common occurrence, and many take anger to bed
but Joy has a Light that illuminates Love, and Love is a seeker of anger
the knowledge of Love breaks the seal of understanding, and he who understands has wisdom.

Intro

Sometimes you fall in love with the one person that nobody else wants you to be with, but you can't control whom you love, and you certainly can't let other people tell you whom to be with. That person just might be the only person in the world that understands you. Only time will tell, but you might actually be better off with that person than with anyone else.

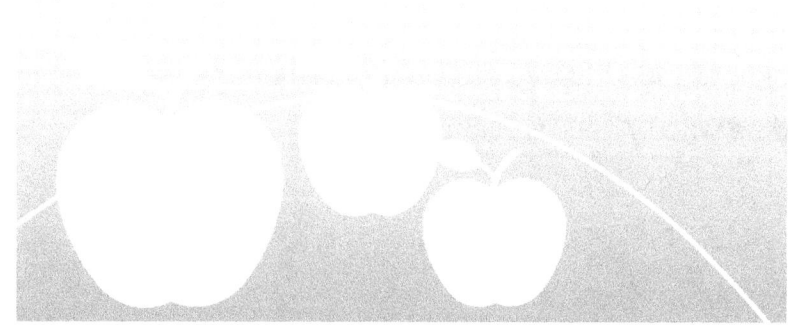

Forbidden Fruit

From the basket you were picked after great deliberation
Beautiful to the sight like you could light up a life
Right for the feel you were firm and fit
Bought for a price you'll never forget

Committed for life with a wife's ambition
In just a few nights you changed my mission
Uncovered my needs, showed the world my greed
Brought me to my knees right in front of my seeds

Forbidden fruit, I fancy you
So why not dance until the dance is through
The world might know, but I don't care
So I'm taking my chance while I'm still here
You are forbidden, but never forget that you are loved...

Intro

When she's out on her own, she might not need you, but a word from you might mean the world to her. She's your queen, and she will always deserve your attention. Be mindful of that and send her a few words.

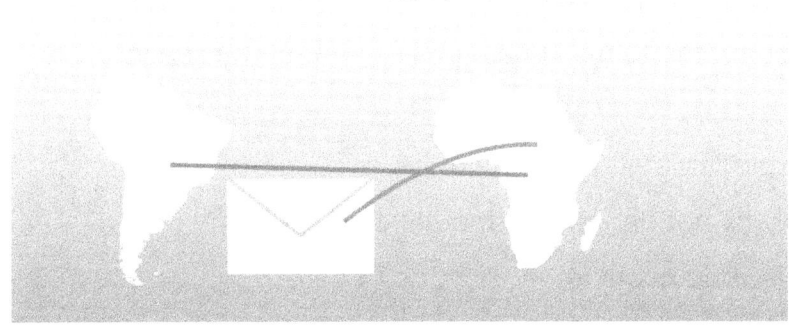

Letter to the Queen

When we are together, you carry yourself like a queen; You behave like one, you think like one
You have a queen's ambition, you dream like a queen

Within a king's thoughts
I pray that you have all of your desires
physical, emotional, spiritual and psychological

Whatever your destiny, I hope your surroundings and everything around you, make you feel like the queen that you are

Forever fulfilled in all aspects of life and love, with companionship dripping in emotional and physical satisfaction.

Be you. Be strong. Be wise. Be ready.
I love you.

Intro

If it was up to them, I would be forced to keep their secrets forever, but it's not, so I'm going to tell everyone what they did to me. I'm telling and so should you.

Broken Vessel

Sticks and stones, of course they didn't break my bones,
but they definitely broke my spirit
at night I hear it screaming for mercy
yes they hurt me, they called me trash, they called me
names; words that a person should never be called, they
beat me like I had no worth, like I denounced my birth, like it
was nothing more than an accident, I will be what I can be
when I get free,
but today I'm in so much pain

Intro

If I know nothing else about this world, at least I know this: the world is full of people who can't wait until you fail, because they can't wait to say they told you so. I'm not worried about failing because I learn something every time I fail.

Keeping the Crown

There's no greater fall than falling from grace
Even a wise man can fall on his face

And he's a king that needs a dream
And he needs a team that needs a king

He lost his magic in the face of madness
How could a king do something so tragic
But he's still human and he's just a man
And sometimes a man has to adjust his plan

I'm keeping the crown when I go down
Because I'm still a king when you're not around

That's my problem with some of these folks
They think I frown every time they joke

They picked up pieces every time I broke
They had my throat every time I choked
They came my way every time I swayed
Then asked for a cut of every buck I made

But I'm keeping the crown when I go down
No matter who's the best pound for pound
I'll still be the best in my own town
I'm keeping the crown when I go down

Intro

Some people won't listen to you until you pack up your things and walk. No matter how many times you threaten to do so, it won't be real to them, until you actually do it. You can talk until you're blue in the face, or you can let them know you're serious and start packing. That's what I would do.

Prophecy 5

There will come a time when you won't even excite me, like maybe, crazy it sounds but when the town burns down the people around won't even notice the flames

Shame on me for trying so long, for crying so long
for lying so long to myself
accept what I offer you and live with it you say
but there will come a day when you can have what you offer,
eat what you don't offer, and swallow what you might

Tonight my feelings bow down to me on command, because where I stand the sand is quick plus thick enough to swallow us both, broken teardrops and cracked eyes shall be no more

I see three candle sticks out in the rain
two still burn but one's in pain
explain I might, but tonight I write this evidence to the future

There will come a time when you won't even excite me, strike me God if I lie, I spread my wings in the night with you, yet I always have to fight with you, you know me, I'm clean

I wash myself and I try again, I'm quick to stand in my sinking sand, yet I go down with you once again

You see a man is just a simple tool, to some a simple fool, your school is no longer in session, so I can't teach you another thing, another bird at another spring told me to use other means to get across to you, I've walked with you through trail ways of never ending missions, so listen to the birds as they sing my song from the trees beyond, or try

I see three candle sticks out in the cold, one don't burn so the rest are cold, explain I could
you wish I would, but this time I'm gone for good

Intro

It's never good to be undertrained. Most people know that, but I question if they know how bad it is to be overtrained. Being over prepared for battle is just as dangerous as being underprepared. All is fair in love and war, so no one cares about how hard you trained. All they care about is winning the battle. One wrong decision can put you in the hands of the enemy, where you will surely meet your demise.

In the Enemy's House

And it came to pass, that I Malachi, blessed by God through faith in Jesus Christ that I may receive salvation, went into the house of the enemy to witness and give testimony.

With my eyes focused and my ears in tune, I entered the dwelling of a friend who knew not the Lord; knowing and believing that the Lord could save him as he saved me. When the time came, I made my move and began to talk about what God had done for me, and he sat and listened in disbelief.

Like anyone hearing of something for the first time, he had questions, which I welcomed, because I had answers. And behold, overwhelming emotions fell upon him and he began to believe that there could be a loving god that controls all things.

But then it came, a question that came not from him, but from the keeper of the house; he that twirleth the double-edged sword with the golden handle that presseth "In this hour" in his palm, and "In that hour" against his fingers. I could hear the roar of a lion, and it paralyzed me so, that I was unable to answer the question.

I remembered something that my teacher once told me about the lion, and what to do if I was fortunate enough to hear it's roar. He told me to retreat into the storehouse, where I keep all my weapons, and use one of them to scare away the enemy.

Well, when the enemy gave chase, I ran towards the storehouse, and when I opened the door there was a great number of weapons, all of which would have worked on the enemy.

But it was this great number that unexpectedly distracted me and caused me to pause for a few seconds. I couldn't decide which weapon to use. And it was during those few seconds that the lion came upon me with overwhelming speed and devoured all that I was and all that I would have been in the life of my friend.

Now I tell everyone I teach, that there may be many weapons in the storehouse, or in other words, there may be many verses in one's memory bank that will work against the enemy, but it is best to use one that is all powerful, but simple; like the name of Jesus.

During spiritual warfare, one cannot afford to pause or freeze up, not even for a few seconds. So I encourage every pupil, every student, and every beginner to carry the name, Jesus, with them into battle, for it is the weapon of the wise.

Intro

Sometimes I wonder if scientists are even trying to find a cure. Maybe the definition of the word cure has changed, or maybe what we used to call a cure no longer exist. I'm starting to believe that it's more profitable to look for a cure than it is to actually find one.

Evasive

My medicine, her medicine and yours
Intertwined in this twisted plot
Men, women and children alike
All begging for an additional shot

Syringes and capsules packed with power
Designed to buy us some time
My days are measured in milligrams
I have nothing but time on my mind

I'm watching the clock, ready to pop
The next pill of the day
Over and over, hour after hour
And no cure is on the way, hmmm...

Intro

You can't deny that there's something going on with today's men. Not all of them need our help but many of them do. They have no idea how much damage they are doing to our world.

Two Cups

And there I was, just sitting there, and with me was a question: "How can a man be willing to take on challengers in the streets, but lack the courage to deal with situations at home with his wife and children?" Why? How? How can this be?

And it came to me: a vision, a vision of two cups. There were two cups, both similar in appearance, and both contained mixes sweet to the taste. But one was sweet to a wise man, and the other sweet to a fool. And one was bitter to a wise man and the other bitter to a fool.

Now the world is confused about which is which and which contains what. So, often, they cheer or show support when a man drinks from the wrong cup. And they often tease or begin to laugh when a man drinks from the right cup. In one cup, there is courage and wisdom, and in the other, anger and pride.

Now a fool is surrounded by a confused world, and it confuses his mind. He believes he drinks from the right cup, but it is the wrong cup all the time. A wise man looks at a battle with courage and wisdom, but a fool looks at a battle with anger and pride. A wise man will walk away from a battle, but a fool will

walk into a trap. A fool has a bold walk, and is seen by the world as courageous. But the world is hungry for ignorance, and what is courageous to the world is unwise.

So, have not courage without wisdom, and have not boldness without faith, because boldness without faith is foolishness, and courage without wisdom is a trap.

Homes are destroyed by anger and pride; either anger <u>and</u> pride, or anger <u>or</u> pride. But those same homes can be rebuilt by courage and wisdom; not courage <u>or</u> wisdom, but courage <u>and</u> wisdom.

In the streets a man can get use to overcoming his challenges with anger; and he can't back down because of his pride. So in order to be victorious at home, he uses the same weapons, and those very weapons often lead to his own undoing.

Intro

I think about it every day. I cry because I know she would cry for me. She loved me more than she loved anyone. She was a mother, a grandmother, a child, a wife, a sister, an aunt and yes, a queen.

The most important Woman to ever Live

When the angels descended, I knew it was time
life would never be the same for this family of mine
when they took her, they took me, I hurt inside
each and every day, I call her name, I still see her face

Her pain is gone, she was oh so strong
she fought for us, she fought so long
I'm sad, but I know she's in a better place
each and every day, I call her name, I still see her face

My tear, my dear, my year, why here
why now, like wow, why this, why now
I'm scared, no fear, she'd say that if she were here
I miss her, I miss her, I miss her,
her...

Intro

It's nice to get what you ask for, but sometimes what you ask for is not what you need. Luxury is not always the answer. Sometimes the worst room in the inn is the best room for you. Sometimes it's not. You need to figure out when to ask for the best and when to let someone else tell you what you really need.

The Innkeeper

There was a certain innkeeper that had three rooms and all were unoccupied. One room had a window to the east, with a view of the rising sun. Another had a window to the west, with a view of the sun setting. The other had no window, nor view, and was the most expensive of them all.

There was an ongoing storm in the land that had already lasted five days and five nights. And there came three men to the inn, each on his own journey. The men wanted to continue home, but all needed shelter from the storm. The first man was a rich man and he asked for the most expensive room. He paid for it with silver and gold, and asked not to be disturbed until after the sun rose again.

The second man was a shepherd, and he paid for his room with cash. And he asked for the room with the window to the west and he was given what he asked.

The third man was a beggar with nothing to give, but he was persistent. And the innkeeper showed him kindness, and did give him a room. And it came to pass, that on the sixth day it

rained and rained, and no one left the inn. On the seventh day the sun did rise, but only one man left the inn. On the seventh evening, the other two men left, one before the other.

The first man who left the inn, found his home unharmed and fled to the high ground. The second man arrived home safe, and eventually did the third. But the land soon slid and destroyed them both, and all that they possessed.

Intro

There's nothing quite like having an affair. I wouldn't recommend it. The grass is rarely greener. The trim is rarely better. It might look better than what you already have, but it's probably not. Stay home and make the best of your situation.

Greener Grass

The grass was green for as far as I could see
And I wanted to be in it as far as I could be
It's my time and her time for me
It's our time and our time to be

It's her dream and she's dreaming of me
I'm not sleep but I'm still in the sheets
I found no peace in the fight for peace
There's no sleep we've been awake for weeks

There's no belly like the belly of the beast
There's no grass like the grass I see
There's no green like the blades I see
She's not crazy just crazy for me

The further I go the more I know
The further we go the less green she show
The further we go the less grass we grow
The further we go the less love she show

I should've stayed home, I should've stayed home
I left my home now I'm all alone

I felt so wrong but I was strong
Her grass was long but felt so wrong

In the grass is where I lost my song
I found my purpose away from home
I left my throne for greener grass
But now I know that it'll never last

Intro

Is it fair for a great, two-term president to be replaced just because he or she can't serve more than two terms. Some people say that it is and some say that it's not, but as for me, I don't swing either way.

The Election

He went through the neighborhood pouring the sauce, like a
thief in the night he was checking them off, stealing the
votes of the ordinary folks
walking the beat, crossing the streets

King of the slums he won over the young
the race was done before it even begun
back again for a second spin
it was clear he was about to win

Did it twice but there could be no third
so he flew away like the bees and birds
we miss him, his guidance and his joyful
personality, bring him back, please

Intro

Some of the most beautiful flowers don't make it through the year. Anybody who's ever planted a garden knows that. Planting a flower at the wrong time is a bad idea, no matter how green you believe your thumb is.

The Virgin

She told me she owed me, but it wasn't true
She was ready to bloom, but it wasn't due
The dew was out and she felt so new
She thought she was ready, but she had no clue

They trampled her petals as they grew
And she didn't gain any medals, so she knew
She made it through spring, summer and fall too
She did everything her momma taught her to do

It was fun while it lasted, but before she knew
Winter came and destroyed everything she knew
She made it back to the rain, but never grew
With all of her beauty, she looked so blue

Intro

The odds are always against us, yet we play like they are not. If we could, we would lose it all for the love of the game and then play the game all over again. We would play and play and play until the game no longer existed, then we would invent the game all over again.

The Casino

The wheels are turning, the money's burning
I'm just learning how to play what's burning
Christmas is coming so I can't be broke
The slots are open, but I'm so broke

If I don't win, it invites the end
Should I lose everything including this Benz
I'm playing my house and maybe my friend's
Maybe my company and maybe my twins

I'm rolling the dice again and again
If I lose I lose, if I win I win
If I lose this game I lose my grin
I hope these folks stop letting me in

Intro

If you know what it's like to be in love with the rudest person on the planet, then you also know what it's like to love the person you hate.

As much as I Hate

There's an inner debate that I can't escape
I wait and I wait but it never takes place
Maybe I love her as much as I hate
Because she's the reason that I fell on my face

I will never get back the time we waste
Maybe I love her as much as I hate
I just can't stomach this inner debate
I wish I knew, but I wait and I wait

I need a new love to help me escape
I wait and I wait for her to come my way
One of these days I'll make my escape
Because maybe I love her as much as I hate
I'm sure of it, I can't stand her

Intro

Pain and suffering is real, especially when a young life is taken away from an expecting mother. I've felt that pain and I know all too well how hard it is to get past it. You never get over it. You never do.

Her

She lost her baby the day it was born

As I lost mine before I even got to know him

I love my baby and she loves her's

I can see her pain in her lost for words

I feel for her as she reflects

She has no clue what she'll do next

I might cry til the day I die

But for her, I hope for a better life

I pray, I wish, I dream,

I feel, I hurt

Intro

Even the worst of us can change. We are not glued to our past mistakes. As long as we have life, we have a chance to change our ways. This could very well be your last chance, so take it and change.

The Road

I'm on a rigid road right in front of my God
And I'm righteous and ready to roar
I wrecked my life like a wretched whore
But I'm renewing my life like I did before

I swore to God I'd be so much more
So I wore what I wore to even the score
I believe in him more with my feet on the floor
But leaving the shore is my Achilles and more

On a rigid road in front of my God
I right my wrongs and do my part
I pay my dues and obey my heart
I work so hard to do my part

Intro

The truth hurts and that's never going to change. I can't change it and neither can you. What we can do though, is see the truth when it's right before our eyes. See it before it's too late. Life is too short to spend it making the same mistake twice.

The Affair

He don't trust her, and she don't trust him
But she trusts me, and he trusts you
Even though none of us can be trusted

I'm not good, and neither are you
But she would do me, and he would do you
Even though none of us can be trusted

He hates her more than she hates him
But he loves you, and you're no gem
I swear none of us can be trusted

She hates him as much as she hates his gem
But she loves me, and I'm no better than them
I'm telling you, none of us can be trusted

Intro

Since the beginning of time people have been doing the unthinkable; they've been stealing kids and tearing families apart. I would love to say that your brother wouldn't do the same, but I can't. The same can be said for your sister, uncle, aunt, mother and your friend — and yes, I would say the same for all of mine, because frankly we have no idea why people do this stuff. The person you least suspect, might be the guilty one.

The Worst

Even the worst words have their place
I'm talking about me, you and hate,
All you do is take
From the playground, schoolyard, amusement park
Whenever you can, whenever you can take,
I hate you

You kidnapper, you thief, you liar, you rapist,
I hate you

I look over my shoulder every day
I can't focus, I can't sleep, I can't play
I can't eat because I hate you

Everywhere I go, I see you trying to steal,
And trying to take,
You and that lady don't deserve to live
I see you taking all these kids
I hate you, today, tomorrow and forever

Intro

These up and down relationships can drive a person insane. I know that because I'm in one. The good times are amazing, but the bad times drive me crazy. If you've been there, then you know what I mean.

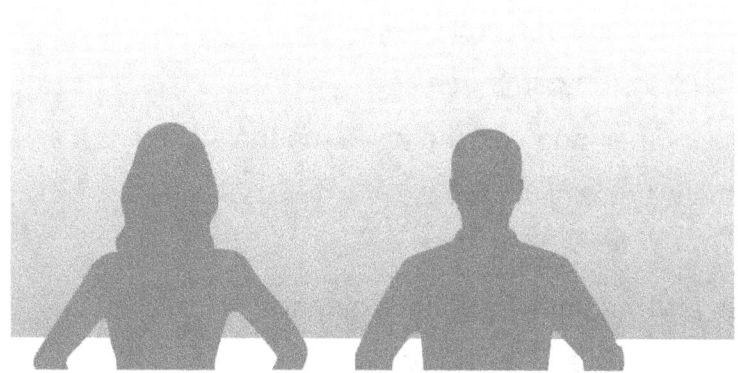

In the midst of battle

She hates me when she hates me,
and loves me when she loves me,
and yes I do the same

We are together forever,
for that I have no shame
It's the way the game goes

I question her and she answers,
that's the way the game goes,
I love loving her, and yes she loves me the same
that's the way the game goes,

We fuss and we fight, and that's alright
because that's just how the game goes

In the midst of battle, the love and hate are one
that's just the way it is,
that's the way the game goes

I'm in then I'm out, she's in without a doubt
because that's how she plays the game

I doubt and I'm out, she fights and pouts

that's the way the game goes

I'm in when she's my friend, but I'm out when that ends,

that's just the way the game goes

Intro

There's nothing quite like a mother's love, but not all mothers love the same. I can name a handful of mothers right now, that would lie on their kids just to get a check. Is that love? I don't think it is.

Greed

If my Grace go get it while the getting is good
I might get me some grain, I might get me an acre or two, I might net a little gain,

Gather some Gin for Grace to guzzle, she might fall for a gimmick or two, pump her up with guilt and grief, I'll be back in a minute or two

I'm going to get my granny glasses, my cane and my giant pills, garnish the table with grapes and greens, you know my Grace will be thrilled

Let's hope Mrs. Geeky and Gullible leaves her brain at the door, but if we can't get it all tonight, we can always get some more

Intro

He loved her and he meant it every time he told her those three words. You know the words. She had him and he had her. Sometimes that's all that matters.

Affection of Perfection

It's like golden lace over the faces of angels in heaven...

I look through clear windows at poses of roses that just keep me hoping that one day, one hour, one rose might be different

I lean on you and you hold me like I've never been held before, you send shockwaves through my new days and make my heart beat again like drums to a man who longs for music as though it was a gift from God

As light as the wind is how I feel when your skin is within my reach again, you send smiles every time you smile and make me wild like forests of rain, your reign as queen of my fantasy island has been piling on years

You're the most beautiful woman walking the face of Mother Earth, every step you take you own your space and take your place

With past memories of perforated love that just rips out, I think about your house of love that's decorated with affection, built on perfection and set alone on an island of common trust

Within you I see all the things I've ever wanted in a woman, and that's the truth, coming from a man that expects a lot from a companion, abandon all of your thoughts of unhappiness and pick up life with me

Let's ride down the highways and byways of eternal peace, piece together our souls and add gold to our thoughts of happiness, reminisce on our past days and lock them in a chest corroded by the underworlds of the sea, be with me and be complete

Intro

There's nothing new under the sun. You'll figure that out as soon as you take your focus off the sparrow. The crazy stuff that happened years ago, is still happening today. It may be wrapped in different packaging, but trust me, it's all the same.

Sparrow

They robbed men of their riches, raped their women, murdered their children, stole their food, burned their houses and slaughtered their horses, all so that they could be king

Out of fear, they fortified their castles, trained their men for war, built up their armories, prayed to the gods and hoped that one of them would show them mercy

For wisdom, they scarified women and children, burned them over an open flame, robbed them of their dignity and embarrassed their families, all so that they could be king

To maintain control, they played politics with commoners, stripped them of their wealth, dared them to rebel and hung everyone who tried

They enslaved a great people, stole them from their families, tossed them in cages, beat them with chains, all so that they could be king, but to this day they still can't see the value of the sparrow, and they never will

Afterword

The stories of rape, incest, molestation, and abuse are all stories from my own life, but I could not express them as such. For a long time I blocked them from my memory, but then they came to me in the most unusual way; they came in the form of someone else's reality, and not my own. Mentally, I could handle them that way, but I still couldn't talk about them. I simply wasn't strong enough. I couldn't accept them as my own experiences, so I pretended like they belonged to someone else. Pages of Life was written through the eyes of others to support those who are still too hurt to speak for themselves. To those of you who are struggling, I am with you. My hope is that you will keep turning your pages until you are strong enough to deal with them.

Guide

About Yesterday, Today

Shine bright -
Because tonight's the night to excite the knight...**pg 24**

The Affair

He don't trust her, and she don't trust him
But she trusts me, and he trusts you...**pg 154**

Affection of Perfection

It's like golden lace over the faces of angels in heaven
I look through clear windows at poses of roses that...**pg 163**

Almost Gone

Would you rather be a lonely lady for a simple reason, or a lonely man in a plentiful season... **pg 107**

Anastasia

I was a superhero when I was five,
With my mother's eyes and my father's pride...**pg 2**

And You

...and You
...and you are like spring water flowing over my life...**pg 32**

As clear as Day

Picture perfect, pretty babe
Precious, priceless loving grace...**pg 94**

As much as I Hate

There's an inner debate that I can't escape
I wait and I wait but it never takes place...**pg 148**

Blue Birds

Blue birds shadowed a shallow land
Ungrateful in fashion for friendly hands...**pg 45**

Book of Dreams

Life is like a book of dreams

Trapped in a cave near a red river stream...**pg 42**

The Breath

I was holding my chest tight,

As tight as a chest could be held...**pg 11**

Broken Vessel

Sticks and stones, of course they didn't break my bones,

but they definitely broke my spirit...**pg 117**

The Casino

The wheels are turning, the money's burning

I'm just learning how to play what's burning...**pg 146**

Dinner with a wise Man
as a wise Man sees a Star

Open my mind and sip fine wine

and watch time rewind back to a time...**pg 7**

Dissatisfaction

Sit down,

and feel the terror and horror in the area of love...**pg 38**

The Election

He went through the neighborhood pouring the sauce, like a thief in the night he was checking them off...**pg 142**

The Essence of Everything

The misty sky before a busy night
Is all I see with you...**pg 4**

Eternity

Eternity is nothing to a king without a queen
One with a voice and no song to sing...**pg 16**

Evasive

My medicine, her medicine and yours
Intertwined in this twisted plot...**pg 129**

Eyes of the Conquered

So great was his sword, his shield, his strength
His men, his might, his plan...**pg 40**

The Fireworks in the Sky

The fireworks in the sky remind me of the first time I saw your face...**pg 65**

Forbidden Fruit

From the basket you were picked after great deliberation
Beautiful to the sight like you could light up a life...**pg 113**

Forever

He died holding my hand and I never caught his name, at twenty-five he died, at church...**pg 9**

Genus

She went through the best of me with her mental telepathy, classified me physically as the god of misery...**pg 68**

Greed

If my Grace go get it while the getting is good

I might get me some grain...**pg 161**

Greener Grass

The grass was green for as far as I could see

And I wanted to be in it as far as I could be...**pg 139**

The Heart that grew a Flower

There was a heart that knew no love,

That had no life, that knew no wife...**pg 60**

Her

She lost her baby the day it was born

As I lost mine before I even got to know him...**pg 150**

Highlighted Flower-Ship

It sailed like a ship of peace, floating across the sea beneath

Brightened by sun rays as is the soul on Sundays...**pg 104**

**The Hunt for Peace
And the joyful Light that loves It**

There is a Light that shines in the darkness, and Darkness himself knows not why…**pg 110**

I don't need You

I don't, because I lost all trust in people
The moment he touched me I knew…**pg 97**

I know Misery

I know misery, it loves company
I see signs of what it's done to me…**pg 92**

The Innkeeper

There was a certain innkeeper that had three rooms and all were unoccupied. One room had a window to the…**pg 136**

In the Enemy's House

And it came to pass, that I Malachi, blessed by God through faith in Jesus Christ that I may receive salvation…**pg 125**

In the midst of battle

She hates me when she hates me,
and loves me when she loves me…**pg 158**

Just after Five

Pronounced dead at five seventeen
her cries never heard through her mother's screams…**pg 63**

Keeping the Crown

There's no greater fall than falling from grace
Even a wise man can fall on his face…**pg 119**

Letter to the Queen

When we are together, you carry yourself like a queen; You behave like one, you think like one…**pg 115**

The lost Letter

The letter Love was in the language of Lust,

Silently lurking – longing to be learned...**pg 14**

Lost near the Lonely

I feel your love, it's oh so grand,

But bland to a man who fails to understand...**pg 22**

Magnificent Cup

Don't rush through life

You might fall off the moon...**pg 19**

Mirror to my Soul

Now within these thoughts, my mind switches over

my clover lacking a leaf, my leaf missing a stem...**pg 99**

Misconception

I'm not a man of many faces

so people want to hurt me just to see me hurt...**pg 28**

The Mist that covered the Window

As the moon released the sky,
and the sun drew it in...**pg 54**

**The most important Woman
to ever Live**

When the angels descended, I knew it was time
life would never be the same for this family of mine...**pg 134**

Mountain of Hope

As white tears came down the mountain
Roaring loud as heck...**pg 89**

Othella

This Sabbath day is a time of truth,
My ancient queen in this time of youth...**pg 101**

Pages of Life

Why must they judge a book by its cover?
When they can flip through the pages of birthdays...**pg 83**

Prophecy 5

There will come a time when you won't even excite me, like maybe, crazy it sounds but when the town burns...**pg 122**

The Road

I'm on a rigid road right in front of my God
And I'm righteous and ready to roar...**pg 152**

Saturation

Specs and pixels, dots and spots
A digital love affair that's heated-hot...**pg 30**

Say no More

She said it was beautiful, and I wished her well,
She threw three or four pennies in the wishing well...**pg 81**

The Seven Wonders of the World

When I look in your eyes I see butterflies that land on piles of sand, sat down by angel men, flew in from heaven...**pg 51**

The Shame

I'll give you some candy he said, as he climbed up on my back, but candy just wasn't good enough...**pg 70**

Sleeping without a Wife

The move she made created distance –
Emotional space in the face of need...**pg 26**

Slipping

He was slipping that's for sure
But she was on a ship headed for shore...**pg 78**

Some kind of Love Poem

Your eyes and your face is a beautiful place
For me to look and write some kind of love poem...**pg 75**

Sparrow

They robbed men of their riches, raped their women, murdered their children...**pg 166**

Success is in the Apple Trees

First, he looked up high
Then, he looked down low...**pg 72**

The Thorn in my Side

I should have a crown on my head,
But instead, I have a thorn in my side...**pg 57**

Through the Eyes of an abandoned Few

I see you world, as broken glass
You spilled my hopes and dreams...**pg 48**

Today's Market

Roses are red, violets are blue –
Gist of the things we used to do...**pg 34**

Two Cups

And there I was, just sitting there, and with me was a question: "How can a man be willing to take on...**pg 131**

Vigilante

You might say it was a justifiable homicide, or just another day when the junkie died...**pg 36**

The Virgin

She told me she owed me, but it wasn't true
She was ready to bloom, but it wasn't due...**pg 144**

Where is my special Someone?

There he is, somewhere far down the road
Right between fate and fantasy...**pg 86**

The Worst

Even the worst words have their place
I'm talking about me, you and hate...**pg 156**

Acknowledgements

Thank you to all of you who inspired me to write the poems in this collection. Without inspiration from you, the words in this book would've been hard to come by. The experiences that we shared together will never be forgotten, which is why I owe you a tremendous amount of gratitude.

About the Author

Born in the small town of Clarksdale, Mississippi, Calvin Morris always believed that he could defy the odds and become an award-winning poet. But first, he had to fight his way through stints of homelessness, abuse and molestation. His real life experiences have given him the ability to create timeless, thought-provoking poems that embed themselves in the hearts of readers.

Connect with others who share your love for poetry at https://m.facebook.com/mypagesoflife/. Feel free to share your thoughts about Pages of Life with others on our page. I would love to hear how you feel about the poems in this collection. Recommend Pages of Life to your friends and encourage them to leave a review. Every review is another page in the life of a poet.

Pages of Life

A Poetry Collection by

Calvin D. Morris

The End

www.ingramcontent.com/pod-product-compliance
Lightning Source LLC
Chambersburg PA
CBHW052028070526
44584CB00016B/1954